PLANET EARTH
DISCOVERIES

by TAMRA B. ORR

CAPSTONE PRESS
a capstone imprint

Smithsonian is published by Capstone Press
1710 Roe Crest Drive North Mankato, Minnesota 56003
www.mycapstone.com

Library of Congress Cataloging-in-Publication Data
Names: Orr, Tamra, author.
Title: Planet Earth discoveries / by Tamra B. Orr. Description: North Mankato,
Minnesota : Capstone Press, [2018] | Series: Smithsonian. Marvelous
discoveries | Audience: Ages 7–10. Identifiers: LCCN 2018006058 (print) |
LCCN 2018010920 (ebook) | ISBN 9781543526264 (eBook PDF) | ISBN
9781543526189 (hardcover) | ISBN 9781543526226 (pbk.) Subjects: LCSH:
Technological innovations--Juvenile literature. | Inventions—Juvenile
literature. | Science—Miscellanea—Juvenile literature. Classification: LCC
T173.8 (ebook) | LCC T173.8 .O745 2018 (print) | DDC 600—dc23
LC record available at https://lccn.loc.gov/2018006058

Editorial Credits
Michelle Hasselius, editor; Heidi Thompson, designer;
Svetlana Zhurkin, media researcher; Kris Wilfahrt, production specialist

Our very special thanks to Don E. Wilson, Curator Emeritus, Vertebrate
Zoology, at the National Museum of Natural History for his review. Capstone
would also like to thank the following at Smithsonian Enterprises: Kealy
Gordon, Product Development Manager; Ellen Nanney, Licensing Manager;
Brigid Ferraro, Vice President, Education and Consumer Products; and Carol
LeBlanc, Senior Vice President, Education and Consumer Products.

Photo Credits
CDC: Melissa Dankel, 15 (bottom); Library of Congress, 15 (top); NASA:
MODIS Rapid Response Team, cover; Newscom: FeatureChina/Xi Li, 6,
picture-alliance/dpa/ScanPyramids Mission, 8, picture-alliance/dpa/
ScanPyramids Mission/Philippe Bourseiller, 5, Reuters/Brian Snyder, 14–15,
Science Photo Library/steve gschmeissner, 17, Science Photo Library/
Victor Habbick Visions, 18–19, TNS/Bay Area News Group/John Green,
16; Optoelectronics Research Centre: Professor Peter Kazansky, 22–23; Prof.
Evelyn N. Wang, MIT, 25; San Jose University: Craig Clements, 26; Science
Source: David Gifford, 18 (left), Sinclair Stammers, 7; Shutterstock: alexkoral,
24, Bestweb, 28, bygermina (circuit tree), 2–3 and throughout, chuyuss, 29,
Elena Pavlovich, 13 (top), EQRoy, 10, hamdan, 9, Jan Kvita, 11, Jerry Horbert,
13 (bottom), Keith Homan, 13 (right), Monkey Business Images, 4, Susanna
D'Aliesio, 12, Tom Reichner, 27; UC San Diego Jacobs School of Engineering: 20
(top), J. Warner, 21, W. Zhu and J. Li, 20 (bottom); University of Minnesota, 19

Quote Sources
Page 23, "Eternal 5D Data Storage Could Record the History of Humankind."
18 February 2016. University of Southampton. https://www.southampton.
ac.uk/news/2016/02/5d-data-storage-update.page

Page 29, "Electric Rain? Solar Panel Turns Raindrops into Power." 11 April
2016. Fox News. http://www.foxnews.com/tech/2016/04/11/electric-rain-
solar-panel-turns-raindrops-into-power.html

Printed in the United States
PA017

TABLE OF CONTENTS

PUTTING TOGETHER THE CLUES

Scientific discoveries are being made almost every day. But often they are just single clues that help solve much bigger mysteries later on. Scientific breakthroughs can come when you least expect them. But the most amazing discoveries happen through patience and hard work.

In 2016 researchers installed a machine that used cosmic rays to scan inside an Egyptian pyramid.

CAPTURED IN AMBER

When you go to the market, you expect to find fruits and vegetables. But what about a dinosaur? In 2016 paleontologist Xing Lida went to a market in Myanmar and discovered a dinosaur's tail.

The tail was inside a small piece of amber. Lida studied the tail and found that the dinosaur's bones, soft tissue, and feathers had all been preserved inside. It's the most complete dinosaur tail ever found. It's about 99 million years old. Experts believe the tail is from a small dinosaur called a Coelurosaur.

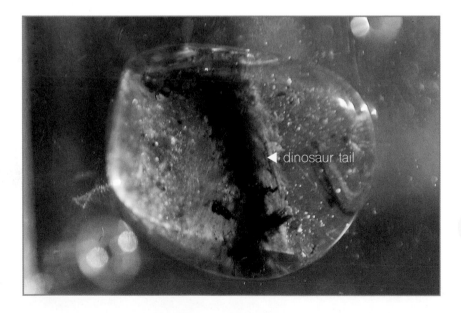

◄ dinosaur tail

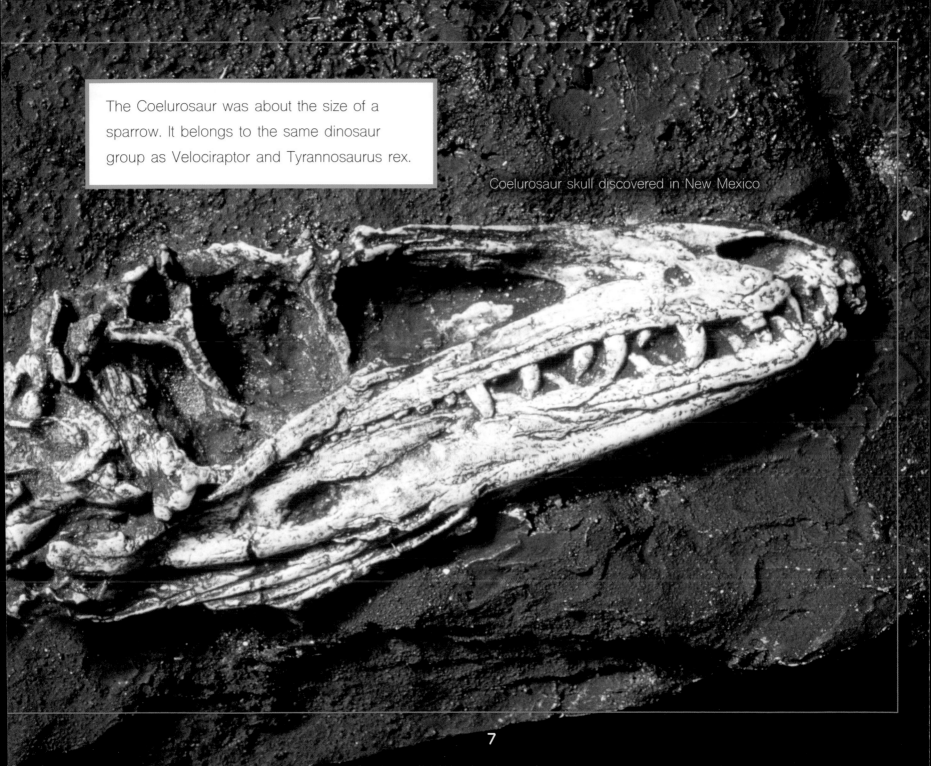

The Coelurosaur was about the size of a sparrow. It belongs to the same dinosaur group as Velociraptor and Tyrannosaurus rex.

Coelurosaur skull discovered in New Mexico

THE GREAT PYRAMID

Imagine finding a room that no one has seen for more than 4,500 years. That is what a group of international researchers did in 2017. They discovered a hidden chamber inside the Great Pyramid in Giza.

The team used cosmic rays to scan the pyramid. These rays can go through stone and show hidden spaces without having to go inside the pyramid. The chamber is about 100 feet (30.5 meters) long. It's still a mystery what the chamber was used for. Scientists plan to build a tiny robot to explore the chamber.

Big Void

Grand Gallery

North Face Corridor

The chamber is the first new structure discovered in the Great Pyramid since the 1800s.

The Great Pyramid was built for Pharaoh Khufu from 2580 to 2560 BC.

The Great Pyramid is 450 feet (137 m) high and 750 (229 m) feet wide. It is considered one of the seven wonders of the ancient world.

THE OLDEST ART

More than 50 years ago, cave paintings were discovered on Sulawesi Island in Indonesia. There were handprints and paintings of large piglike animals called babirusas. At the time, scientists thought they were about 12,000 years old.

Some of the first prehistoric paintings were found in 1880 in the Altamira cave in Spain.

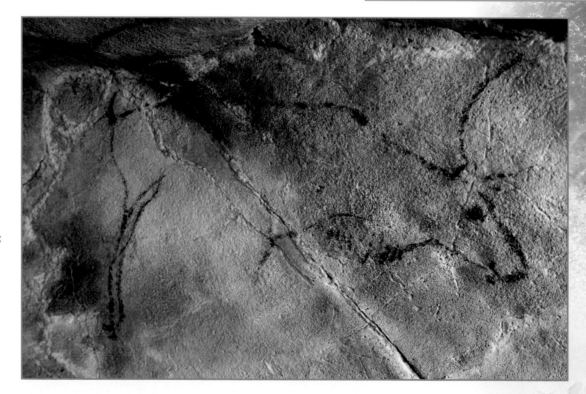

A replica of the prehistoric rock art found in the Altamira cave is on display at the National Museum and Research Center of Altamira.

In 2016 Australian scientists were able to date the paintings using new technology. They determined that the handprints are at least 39,900 years old. This means that they are the oldest known hand tracings in the world.

No one knows why people painted on cave walls. Some scientists believe it was a way to send messages to others.

There were 26 red handprints and a painting of a large boar in the cave in South Sulawesi.

SUPER WHEAT

For years, scientists have tried to find a way to grow more wheat at a faster rate. More wheat means more food to feed people around the world. In 2016 researchers in the United Kingdom were able to change the wheat so that it could use sunlight more effectively. This super wheat grows 15 to 20 percent faster than regular wheat. The U.K. government has approved planting this new crop. In the future, scientists hope to create a super wheat that will not be affected by chemicals.

Wheat was created more than 10,000 years ago from a blend of grass and ancient grains.

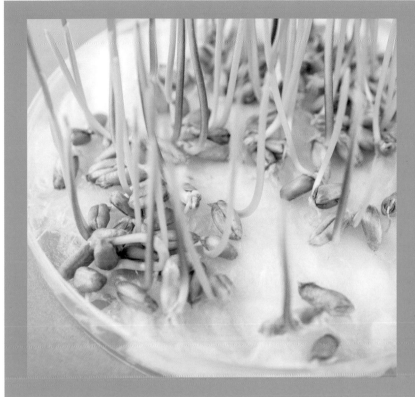

GMOS

Super wheat is a genetically modified organism, or GMO. GMOs are plants, animals, and other organisms that have had their basic makeup changed in some way. For example, scientists have injected strawberries and tomatoes with fish genes to keep the fruits from freezing. Some people think that GMOs will solve many of the world's food problems. Others believe the GMOs are less nutritious or will affect a person's health. Currently 64 countries require GMO foods to be clearly labeled on their packaging.

Some cotton crops have been modified so that they cannot be destroyed by insects.

A NEW ANTIBIOTIC

In 1929 scientist Alexander Fleming discovered penicillin. Penicillin is an antibiotic, which is a medicine that fights bacterial infections in our bodies. Between 1950 and 1970, scientists created more than 100 types of antibiotics. But a new antibiotic hasn't been developed in more than 30 years.

This all changed in 2017. While studying a soil sample, scientists from Boston's Northeastern University discovered a new antibiotic called teixobactin. Teixobactin is still being studied. But one day scientists hope this new antibiotic will be used to cure serious illnesses, such as pneumonia, tuberculosis, and staph infections.

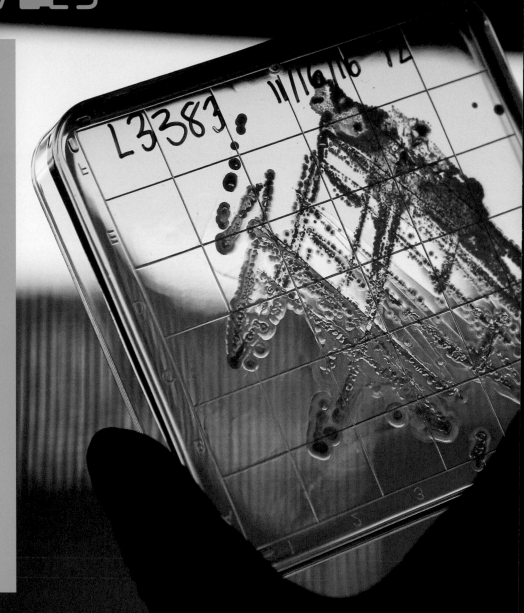

In 2016 a scientist held a sample of *Eleftheria terrae*, a bacteria used to make teixobactin.

Alexander Fleming was given the Nobel Prize in Physiology or Medicine in 1945 for discovering penicillin.

FIGHTING SUPERBUGS

Superbugs are types of bacteria that are so strong, they cannot be destroyed by today's antibiotics. Bacterial infections that resist antibiotics can be deadly. Developing a new antibiotic that fights against these superbugs will help save many lives.

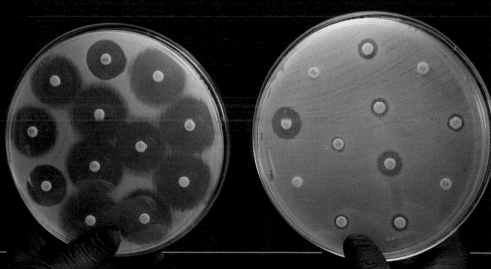

STEM CELLS

Stem cells are cells that have not been assigned a certain job in the body. They can turn into any cells, such as skin cells, liver cells, or blood cells. When we are injured or sick, our stem cells help repair the damage done to our bodies.

Scientists are studying stem cells that have been developed in labs. These cells have been used to treat serious diseases, such as Alzheimer's and Parkinson's. In 2016 a team from Stanford University in California injected these cells into the brains of stroke patients who could not move their limbs. The team discovered that the stem cells helped these patients move again. Some were even able to get out of their wheelchairs and walk!

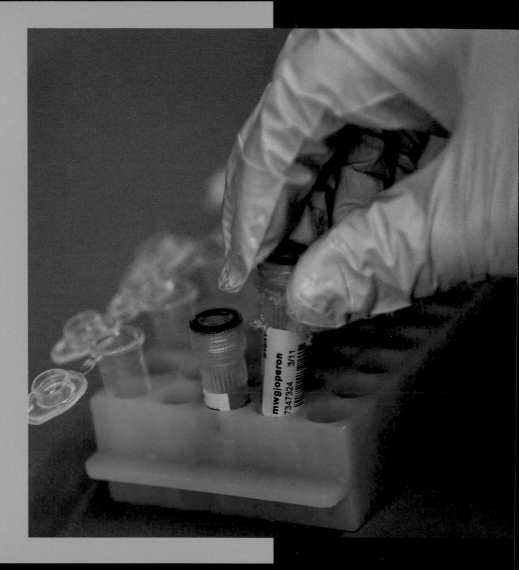

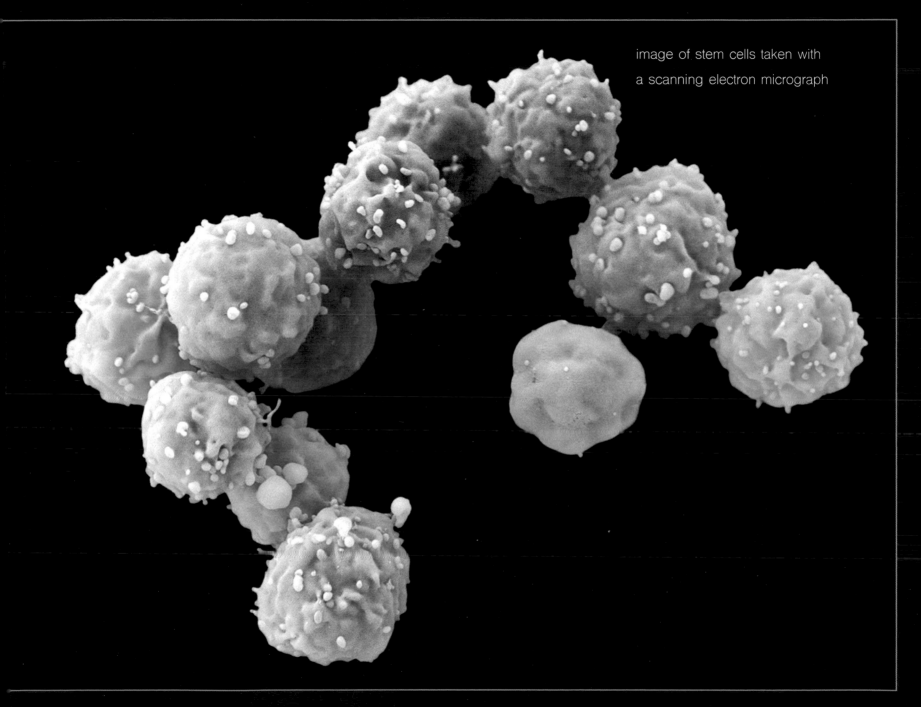

image of stem cells taken with
a scanning electron micrograph

MICROMEDICINE

NANOBOTS

One day you may not have to swallow a pill to take your medicine. It could be delivered by a tiny robot inside your body.

Scientists can program nanobots to move and go. In January 2015 scientists injected nanobots into a live mouse to help cure an ulcer. They programmed the bots to attach to the mouse's stomach wall and deliver the medicine. In the future, doctors may be able to use nanobots on humans.

One day nanobots could destroy cancer in the human body.

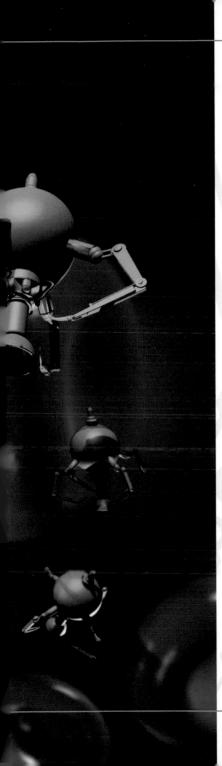

ROBOTIC THOUGHTS

Can you move a robot with your mind? Eight volunteers were asked to do just that at the University of Minnesota in Minneapolis. Researchers asked each volunteer to wear a cap that was fitted with special electrodes. While wearing the cap, the volunteer could move a robotic arm just by thinking about it. Researchers hope that one day this new technology will help people who are paralyzed.

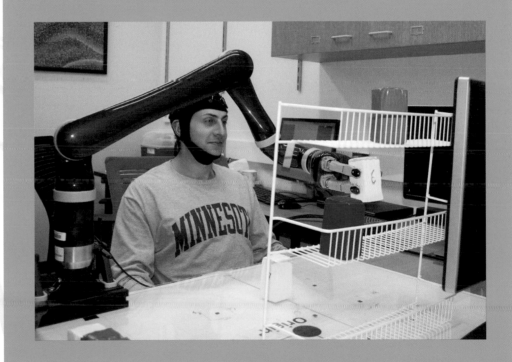

MICROFISH

Tiny fish-shaped robots may help make patients feel better one day. In 2016 researchers from the University of California San Diego created microbots using a 3D printer. The microbots looked like tiny fish.

By using a magnet, a doctor can guide the microfish through a patient's bloodstream to deliver medicine. In the future these fish could be used to get rid of viruses in the body. Others could deliver medicine directly into a tumor or to a part of the body that can't be operated on. Scientists believe that microfish could help people with serious conditions, such as cancer, Hepatitis C, and Parkinson's disease.

Researchers Jinxing Li (left) and Wei Zhu (right) created the microfish.

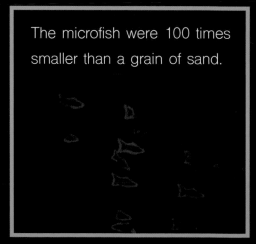

The microfish were 100 times smaller than a grain of sand.

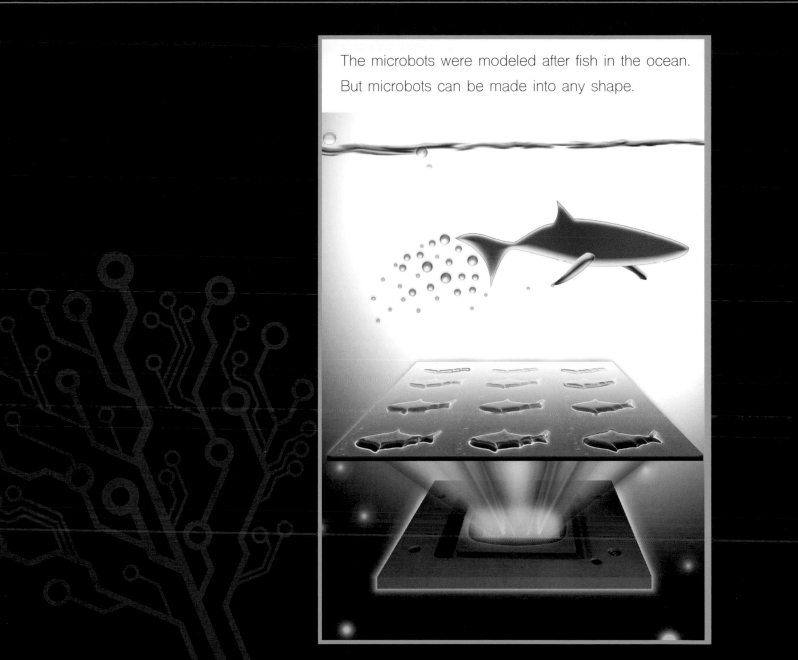

The microbots were modeled after fish in the ocean.
But microbots can be made into any shape.

DATA DISCS

Scientists have created a glass disc that can store huge amounts of information for billions of years. And it's only the size of a quarter. In 2013 researchers from the University of Southampton in the United Kingdom used a laser to write data onto the disc.

The glass discs are made to withstand up to 1,800 degrees Fahrenheit (982 degrees Celsius).

"It is thrilling to think that we have created the technology to preserve documents and information and store it in space for future generations. ... all we've learned will not be forgotten."

—professor Peter Kazansky

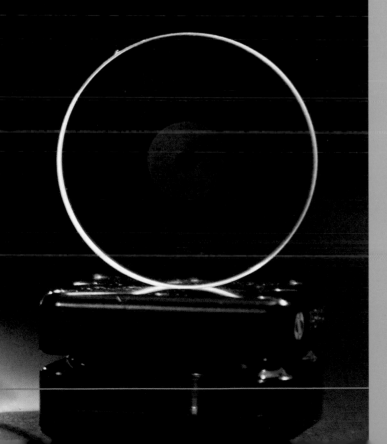

The glass disc can hold 360 terabytes of data. That's almost 3,000 times more information than a regular CD. These discs will make it possible for libraries, museums, and other places that have large records to store information for generations to come.

All 788,258 words of the *King James Bible* were put on one data disc.

THE WATER HARVESTER

Many countries around the world struggle to find clean water. Discovering inexpensive, simple ways to get water has been a top priority for many researchers. In 2017 a team from the Massachusetts Institute of Technology and the University of California created a water harvester. This spongelike machine collects water vapor from the air—even in the driest areas.

The water harvester is solar-powered, so all it needs is sunlight or another source of heat to work. At night the harvester is left open to allow air to flow inside. The air contains water molecules. During the day the machine is closed. The sun turns the water molecules into vapor, and the water is collected.

In the past other machines have been created to collect water from the air. But they need certain types of weather to work properly, such as fog or dew.

The water harvester is able to collect about 3 quarts (2.8 liters) of water a day. That's enough to give one person drinking water for one day.

WILDFIRE WEATHER

Wildfires are devastating. These fires kill plants and animals and can spread from forests into areas where people live. In 2017 scientists from San Jose State University in California discovered that wildfires can also change the weather. Wind created by the fires changes the area's temperature.

The scientists had to take firefighter training to get close enough to the wildfires to get data. They have studied about 24 wildfires across the western United States so far.

In 2017 scientists collected data from the Detwiller wildfire in California.

In 2015 the Okanogan Complex wildfire in Washington destroyed acres of land and more than 100 homes. It is one of the biggest wildfires in the state's history.

In 2015 there were 68,151 wildfires throughout the United States. The fires burned 10.1 million acres of land.

RAINDROP POWER

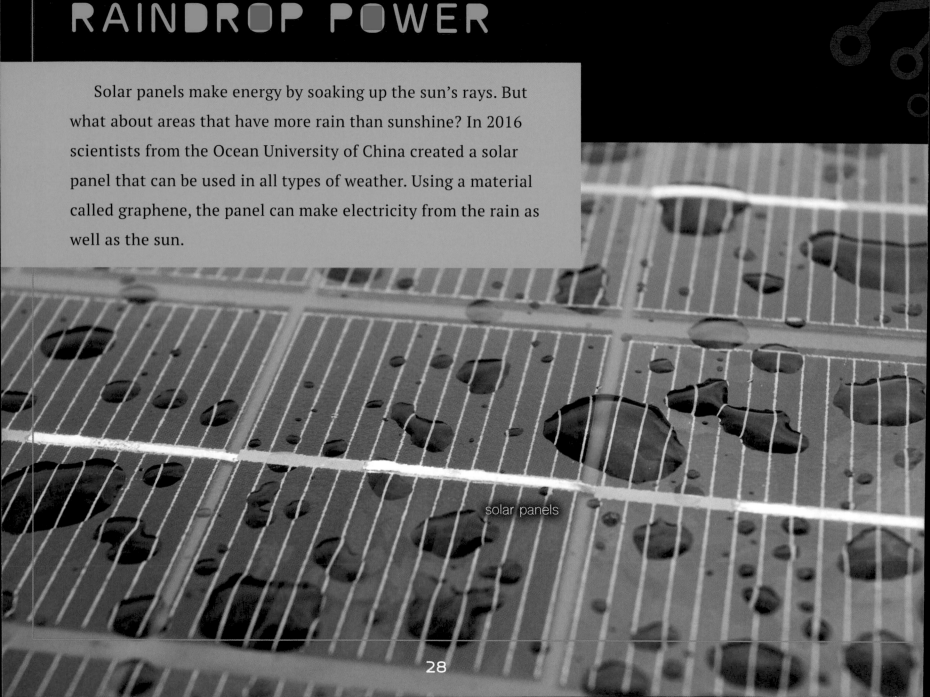

Solar panels make energy by soaking up the sun's rays. But what about areas that have more rain than sunshine? In 2016 scientists from the Ocean University of China created a solar panel that can be used in all types of weather. Using a material called graphene, the panel can make electricity from the rain as well as the sun.

solar panels

"We believe the all-weather solar cell will be used for families in [the] future."

— Qunwei Tang, scientist at the Ocean University of China

In 2017 about 2 percent of the electricity in the United States came from solar panels.

GLOSSARY

amber (AM-buhr)—a yellowish brown substance formed from fossilized tree sap; some fossils are preserved in amber

antibiotic (an-ti-bye-OT-ik)—a drug that kills bacteria and is used to cure infections and disease

bacteria (bak-TEER-ee-uh)—very small living things that exist all around you and inside you; some bacteria cause diseases

cosmic ray (KOZ-mik RAY)—a particle traveling through space at a speed approaching that of light

electrode (e-LEK-trode)—a conductor through which electricity enters or leaves an object

gene (JEEN)—a tiny unit of a cell that determines the characteristics that a baby gets from his or her parents

infection (in-FEK-shun)—an illness or disease caused by germs such as bacteria

nanobot (NAN-oh-baht)—a small, self-propelled robot

organism (OR-guh-niz-uhm)—a living thing such as a plant, animal, bacterium, or fungus

paleontologist (pale-ee-uhn-TOL-uh-jist)—a scientist who studies ancient life forms

paralyzed (PA-ruh-lized)—unable to move or feel a part of the body

solar panel (SOH-lur PAN-uhl)—a flat surface that collects sunlight and turns it into power

stem cell (STEM SELL)—type of cell that can give rise to any other kind of cell

stroke (STROHK)—a medical condition that occurs when a blocked blood vessel stops oxygen from reaching the brain

terabyte (TAYR-uh-byte)—a measure of large amounts of data; one thousand gigabytes

water vapor (WAH-tur VAY-pur)—water in gas form; water vapor is one of many invisible gases in air

wildfire (WILDE-fire)—an uncontrolled fire that spreads quickly over woodlands or brush

CRITICAL THINKING QUESTIONS

1. The Great Pyramid of Giza is one of the seven wonders of the ancient world. Describe another one of these wonders.

2. How could a robotic arm help people who are paralyzed?

3. In your own words, describe how the water harvester collects water.

READ MORE

Rooney, Anne. *You Wouldn't Want to Live Without Antibiotics!* You Wouldn't Want to Live Without. New York: Franklin Watts, 2015.

Scibilia, Jade Zora. *Solar Panels: Harnessing the Power of the Sun.* Powered Up! A STEM Approach to Energy Sources. New York: Powerkids Press, 2018.

Stanborough, Rebecca. *The Great Pyramid of Giza.* Engineering Wonders. North Mankato, Minn.: Capstone Press, 2016.

INTERNET SITES

Use FactHound to find Internet sites related to this book.

Visit *www.facthound.com*

Just type in 9781543526189 and go.

Check out projects, games and lots more at
www.capstonekids.com

INDEX